# Divine Healing Vision

*The Art of Soul Love*

**Jaya Sarada**

© 2025 Jaya Sarada All rights reserved.

No part of this publication may be reproduced, distributed, or transmitted in any form or by any means, including photocopying, recording, or other electronic or mechanical methods, without the prior written permission of the author, except in the case of brief quotations used in reviews or critical commentary.

Printed in the United States of America.

ISBN: 978-1-893037-38-0

The dove symbolizes peace and spirit; the rose represents love and beauty. Together, they signify peaceful, pure, and divine love.

# Dedication

A heartfelt offering to the Divine, seekers of light, and all who awaken to love.

### Embracing the Sacred Path

The Divine Healing Vision journey highlights trust, presence, and surrender. This sacred invitation encourages you to slow down and develop deeper awareness, honoring each step as vital to your growth. By practicing patience and openness, you make room for intuition to thrive and true transformation to happen.

In this mindful presence, the journey becomes a living process—one where self-discovery and divine connection intertwine. Core practices of presence, soul embodiment, and divine alignment serve as pillars supporting your ongoing spiritual growth. Through reflective questions and practical exercises, you are encouraged to actively participate in your healing process. By observing, listening, and practicing, you incorporate these teachings, fostering wholeness and illuminating your path with clarity, love, and light.

### Alignment with Divine Essence

Transformation happens naturally when you connect with your divine self. Each chapter provides an opportunity to pause, breathe, and tune into your inner sanctuary. Trust the universe's support, knowing that every insight, breath, and intention plants seeds for miracles to grow. This guide helps you awaken to your highest self, deepen your connection with your soul, and align with the divine flow that directs all life. The insights, practices, and reflections inside support your spiritual growth, healing, and inner transformation.

## Acknowledgments

With heartfelt gratitude, I acknowledge the unseen forces of grace that have guided, inspired, and brought this work into existence. To the teachers, mentors, and messengers of light who have shared wisdom through presence and compassion—thank you for lighting the way.

# Preface

## Entering the Light of Divine Healing Vision

This work gently encourages you to awaken your inner vision, guiding you to recognize and honor the Divine presence within. These pages aim to help you reconnect with your inner sanctuary, fostering deep alignment and spiritual awareness.

Every soul holds an inner memory of divine wholeness—a quiet awareness that it was created from love, by love, and for love. Throughout human life, this memory can become hidden beneath fear, attachment, and illusion. Divine Healing Vision gently encourages you to lift that veil and remember the radiant truth within. This book is not meant to be studied as a lesson but experienced as a living transmission. Each chapter guides you on a sacred journey—from awakening your inner vision to releasing what no longer serves you and embodying your soul's light in daily life. Read these pages slowly with awareness and openness. Allow the words to connect with your mind, heart, and energy body. Breathe with each reflection, pause after every paragraph, and embrace the silence between sentences as part of the experience.

This work combines prayer, insight, and practical spiritual guidance to help you reconnect with your Source. Each concept—vision, intuition, surrender, presence, embodiment—is not just an idea to understand but a frequency to receive. Through stillness and intention, you will start to see with divine eyes: perceiving love where there was once fear, and light where there was once separation.

The journey is circular, not linear. You can revisit any chapter anytime and discover new insights. Healing, transformation, and ascension are ongoing—a gentle unfolding of grace throughout your life. Above all, let this book remind you that the Divine has never been separate from you. The light you seek is the light you are. The guidance you call upon already resides within your sacred heart.

Take a deep breath now. Feel the pulse of divine life flowing through you. This is the beginning — or perhaps the continuation — of your miraculous transformation. Welcome home to the light.

*When you look through divine eyes, every moment turns into a prayer, and every breath—a revelation.*

## Table of Contents

Chapter 1: vision is the language of my soul ................................ 10

Chapter 2: vision as the activity of intuition ................................ 14

Chapter 3: letting go—the art of receiving ................................ 17

Chapter 4: the power of presence in healing ................................ 20

Chapter 5: soul embodiment—fully present in form ................................ 23

Chapter 6: divine alignment of body, mind, and soul ................................ 26

Chapter 7: you are light in motion ................................ 29

Chapter 8: remember your sacred origin ................................ 32

Chapter 9: healing the root cause of separation and illness ................................ 36

Chapter 10: the sacred heart initiation—entering your inner sanctuary ................................ 42

Chapter 11: ascension—your soul's calling ................................ 46

Chapter 12: transformation is the work of a light being ................................ 52

Chapter 13: trusting your source ................................ 57

Chapter 14: witnessing light—living in divine trust ................................ 61

Chapter 15: the art of soul love ................................ 66

Conclusion ................................ 72

*I belong to no religion.
My religion is love. Every
heart is my temple.*

*- Rumi*

# Chapter 1
## vision is the language of my soul

*What my heart can see, creation rushes to meet.*

### The Power of Divine Seeing

Seeing forms the foundation of all manifestation. When your inner vision awakens, you align your thoughts, emotions, and spirit with divine intention. To see is not just to look—it is to recognize the truth already within you. Each moment you hold a pure image of love, healing, or abundance in your heart, that vision manifests in unseen realms.

Energy responds to awareness. Light reacts to focus. Creation unfolds in harmony with your chosen perception. Seeing through divine eyes means perceiving not what seems broken, but what is becoming whole. When you shift your gaze from fear to faith, the world before you rearranges itself to reflect that clarity.

### Awakening Inner Sight

Divine vision starts in silence. Close your external eyes and focus inward. Beneath the chaos of thoughts, you can feel the gentle pulse of creation. Here, imagination becomes a sacred conversation—your soul communicating with the Divine.

Divine Vision unfolds just like dawn replaces night: quietly, naturally, and gracefully. Each time you trust this inner sight, you strengthen the bridge between spirit and matter. Manifestation isn't magic—it's alignment. What you bless with loving attention begins to come into being through you.

**From Seeing to Manifesting**

Once you clearly see the image within, release it into divine flow. Do not cling or question when it will manifest. Trust that creation has already responded to your vision. Your task is to maintain the frequency of belief. Speak life into your vision. Act as if it has already come to pass. Gratitude is the language of manifestation; faith is its rhythm. Remember, manifestation is not about claiming possessions — it is the unveiling of truth. You are not creating something new; you are allowing divine wholeness to reveal itself through your awareness.

**Reflective Questions and Sacred Practices**

Daily Visualization Exercise: Spend five to ten minutes each day visualizing your deepest heartfelt wishes as if they've already come true. Fully engage in these imagined scenarios, intentionally bringing out feelings of gratitude and happiness. Feel the emotions of fulfillment and presence, letting these sensations strengthen your vision.

**Sacred Practice: The Vision Meditation**

- Find a quiet space and sit quietly, taking several deep, calming breaths.

- Bring to mind a vision that lifts your spirit—such as peace, healing, purpose, or love.

- Visualize this vision as a bright, glowing light before you, seeing it as whole and alive.

- Whisper: "I see through divine eyes. What I see in truth is already so."

- Rest in gratitude, trusting that the unseen is unfolding through grace.

**Affirmation:** *"What I see with love becomes real through love. My vision and the Divine create as one."*

**Sacred Practice: The Breath of Release**

- Sit quietly and keep your eyes closed.
- Take a slow, deep breath through your heart, visualizing light filling every cell.
- Exhale softly, releasing all that feels heavy or tight.
- With each breath, repeat: "I release what no longer resonates with me, and I open myself to a new way of being aligned with the Divine."
- Continue for five minutes, ending with gratitude.

**Affirmation:** "By releasing the past and surrendering the future, I stay open to the miracle of this moment."

*In the silence of love, you will
find the spark of life.*

**-Rumi**

# Chapter 2

# vision as the activity of intuition

*I trust my inner knowing to lead me toward my highest purpose.*

**The Power of Inner Guidance**

Divine Healing Vision focuses on intuition, acting as a conduit for revealing the divine plan. This vision encourages you to let go of resistance, allowing clear purpose to surface and highlighting the interconnectedness of all life. As you release resistance, the divine plan unfolds smoothly, bringing a deep sense of peace and fulfillment. Intuition becomes available when you respect the subtle wisdom inside, listen past daily distractions, and trust the gentle nudges of your soul.

Vision goes beyond just physical sight. It offers an intuitive understanding that uncovers deeper meaning and purpose. By tuning into your inner sight, you become aware of patterns and divine guidance woven throughout your life.

**Whispers of the Soul**

Whispers of the soul gently arise beneath conscious thought, guiding you with tender wisdom. As you listen to these inner messages, you strengthen your bond with the sacred rhythm of intuition and surrender. Each delicate whisper invites trust in the unfolding journey, encouraging openness to divine guidance.

**Reflective Questions**

- What subtle guidance has my intuition provided lately?
- Where am I resisting life's flow?
- How can I better listen to my soul's gentle nudges?

**Daily Exercise:** Set aside 5-10 minutes each day to sit quietly in silence. Focus on a question you seek guidance for. Notice the first impressions, subtle feelings, or quiet thoughts that come up. Welcome these insights without judgment.

*Your heart knows the way;
run in that direction.*

*-Rumi*

# Chapter 3
## letting go—the art of receiving

*In the gentle act of releasing, grace flows. In surrender, I become the open vessel through which love moves.*

### The Sacred Practice of Surrender

Letting go is a sacred invitation to receive. When you release attachments and expectations, you create space within yourself for divine blessings. Surrendering is not a sign of weakness; it is a profound act of faith. Each time you relinquish control, you open a channel for light to flow freely through your life.

Letting go isn't about losing; it's about making space. Every breath offers a chance to release what no longer serves your highest good—old habits, lingering fears, or stories that keep you small.

### Trusting the Flow of Divine Order

Facing the unknown takes courage. The mind often resists uncertainty, but the soul understands that every letting go brings renewal. Trust that divine order is always present, even when the path ahead isn't clear.

Letting go becomes a sacred exchange—your willingness for grace. Remember: letting go doesn't mean giving up; it means surrendering—placing your burdens in divine hands and resting in the gentle rhythm of love.

### Receiving Through Openness

The art of receiving starts with an open heart. True receiving involves actively connecting with divine flow. You accept not just material blessings but also peace, wisdom, and joy. Be willing to accept

without guilt or doubt. When divine love offers its gifts, embrace them completely.

**Reflective Questions**

- What am I holding on to that no longer resonates with me?
- How does resisting change hinder my growth?
- What blessings could emerge if I let go of control?

**Exercise: The Ritual of Release**

Identify one thing you're ready to let go of. Please write it down on paper as a conscious act of acknowledgment. With a slow, intentional breath, imagine yourself releasing this burden as you exhale deeply. Visualize it gently leaving your body and dissolving into the air.

As you keep breathing, imagine bright divine light entering the space you've cleared. Feel this light filling you with warmth, peace, and renewal, affirming your openness to receive new blessings.

*A candle never loses any of its light
while lighting another candle.*

*-Rumi*

# Chapter 4

## the power of presence in healing

*I focus on the present moment to foster peace, clarity, and healing.*

### The Essence of Transformation

Transformation occurs when you focus on the present moment. By intentionally releasing past pain and letting go of worries about the future, you create space for healing and clarity. Being present brings peace and renewal, supporting your growth potential.

### The Foundation of Healing

Presence is the foundation of all healing. It encourages you to be fully aware and engaged in each moment. By anchoring your focus in the present, you tap into the transformative power of conscious awareness, nurturing both your body and soul.

In the stillness of being present, healing occurs naturally, guided by the wisdom that emerges when distractions are released and the sacredness of your journey is honored.

**Compassion Through Mindful Observation:** In this mindful state, thoughts and emotions are recognized and observed without becoming overwhelming. Compassion and understanding arise naturally, fostering self-love and acceptance. Each breath reconnects you with your inner wisdom and loving support.

Presence acts as a gateway for divine energy, encouraging growth and renewal. When you are fully aware of each breath and sensation, remarkable miracles can happen.

**Reflective Questions**

- Where do I genuinely exist in my life?
- How can I enhance my loving awareness at each moment?

**Practical Application: Mindfulness Practice**

Spend 5-10 minutes observing your thoughts and physical sensations as they come up. Take deep breaths, letting each one ground you in the present moment. Affirm: "I am fully present, and healing flows through me."

*The heart has its own language. The heart knows a hundred thousand ways to speak.*

*-Rumi*

# Chapter 5

## soul embodiment—fully present in form

*My body, mind, and soul are in harmony. Divine energy flows freely within me.*

**Living Your Highest Truth**

To fully embody your soul means allowing every thought, word, and action to reflect your deepest truth. In this state, your soul's wisdom and authenticity guide your daily choices. This conscious alignment helps you act with integrity.

**Anchoring Divine Essence**

Being fully present in your body honors the sacred connection between spirit and matter, recognizing your body as a vessel for divine energy. Embodiment means filling each moment with purpose, love, and awareness.

As your soul becomes fully embodied, you anchor the divine essence into your physical form. This allows the highest wisdom to guide every thought, word, and action. Through this process, you nurture authenticity, grace, and purpose.

**Living a Soulful Life:** Living as an embodied soul means practicing presence each day, recognizing the sacred in simple moments, and allowing your higher self to guide you through both challenges and joys. By nurturing this connection, you create a sense of wholeness that radiates outward. Every interaction provides an opportunity to share your light by grounding spiritual wisdom in practical, loving ways. This journey isn't about achieving perfection but about embracing both your humanity and divinity as one.

**Reflective Questions**

- How am I expressing my soul in daily life?
- Where can I add more authenticity and elegance?
- Which areas of my life feel disconnected from my soul?
- How can I translate spiritual insights into practical steps?

**Practical Exercises**

**Mindful Movement:** Practice yoga, stretching, or walking meditation. As you move, observe how your body reflects your inner truth, allowing each movement to be a deliberate expression of your soul's wisdom.

**Mindful Daily Task:** Select a routine activity and do it with full awareness. Bring loving intention and mindfulness to turn a simple moment into a chance to embody spiritual presence.

*The only lasting beauty is the beauty of the heart.*

**-Rumi**

# Chapter 6
# divine alignment of body, mind, and soul

*My body, mind, and soul are in harmony. Divine energy moves freely through me.*

**Understanding Divine Alignment**

Divine alignment refers to the harmonious connection between body, mind, and soul. When these parts are in sync, they foster deep well-being, boost energy flow, and enhance clarity and purpose. Taking care of your entire self-lays the groundwork for spiritual growth. Achieving alignment involves constantly refining your thoughts, feelings, and physical presence to match spiritual truth. Practicing this through mindful reflection and gentle exercises promotes clarity, energy, and a renewed sense of purpose.

**Intentional Integration:** When you consciously align your body, mind, and soul, you create space for deep healing and personal growth. This sacred harmony encourages you to listen carefully to every part of yourself—honoring your body's signals, your mind's insights, and your soul's wisdom.

Through mindful practices and gentle self-reflection, you cultivate harmony and balance, enabling each part of your being to support and uplift the others.

**Becoming a Vessel for Divine Energy**

When your body, mind, and soul are in harmony, you become a conduit for divine energy. This radiant sense of well-being inspires others and promotes natural healing and growth.

By intentionally aligning your inner and outer worlds, you unlock new levels of vitality, clarity, and peace. This harmony allows you to

fully embrace your divine potential, radiate light, inspire others, and live in harmony with your soul's purpose.

**Daily Alignment Exercise**

Begin each morning with a quick alignment check:

- Focus on maintaining good posture—stand or sit comfortably, so your body feels balanced.
- Notice your breath—breathe slowly and mindfully a few times to ground yourself.
- Pause to reflect on your thoughts and feelings—kindly recognize what's present without judgment.
- Make minor adjustments as needed to attain balance and calm.

*Would you become a pilgrim on the road of love? The first condition is that you make yourself humble as dust and ashes.*

*-Rumi*

# Chapter 7

## you are light in motion

*I am a shining reflection of divine light, inspiring everyone around me.*

### Embracing Your Light in Motion

Divine alignment is an ongoing journey of conscious growth. It involves attentive listening to your body, honoring your mind's insights, and trusting your soul's guidance.

To embrace your light in motion is to see yourself as a dynamic source of divine energy—continuously growing, shining with your unique brilliance, and influencing those around you. Every step and intention radiates your inner glow, transforming you into a living symbol of hope, inspiration, and possibility.

### Living as Light in Motion

Starting a journey to embody your soul involves living each moment with purpose and love, allowing your spirit to bring deeper meaning to every action. Tuning into your inner wisdom reveals sacredness in everyday experiences, empowering you to shine as your authentic self.

Your light is always unfolding. Every moment presents a fresh opportunity to release divine energy, brighten your path, and inspire others. By living intentionally, you join the continuous flow of creation.

### Reflecting and Embodying Your Light

**Restoring Harmony:** Spot the parts of yourself that feel out of sync. Try an energy scan: sit quietly and focus on the sensations, thoughts, and emotions in your body. As you notice tension, breathe divine light into those areas.

**Radiate Your Inner Light:** Reflect on how you are currently shining your inner light. Practice visualization: imagine your inner light expanding outward, gently reaching everyone you encounter.

**Expressing Your Light:** Practice movement meditation. Whether walking, stretching, or dancing, focus on visualizing your inner light shining outward, touching you and those around you.

*Through love, thorns become roses*

*-Rumi.*

# Chapter 8

# remember your sacred origin

*I am divine, eternal, and complete. I remember my sacred origin.*

### Awakening to Your Soul's Essence

Before your form and life experiences shaped your identity, you existed as pure essence — a spark of Source, untouched by thoughts, conditioning, or emotions. Recognizing this sacred origin awakens the eternal light within and reaffirms your divine heritage.

### The Emergence of Ego

The sense of "I" gradually evolved into the ego—an adaptable structure designed to help you navigate the physical world. Still, the divine light of creation inside you remains untouched. As you shed layers of conditioning, you release limitations and reconnect with your true self—a luminous, free, and expansive soul.

**The Journey Beyond the Veil:** The illusion that caused forgetfulness started when the life force became aware of itself through sensations and external experiences, creating a veil over your sacred origin. Throughout your journey, you have worked to shed the conditioning of the false self and reconnect with your true nature.

**Embracing Your Divine Light:** Deep within your core, the divine light of creation dwells, holding a unique signature and purpose. Your gifts are prepared to be unveiled as you shed layers of conditioning. Your primary task is to rise into the mystical radiance of your soul and become part of the glorious beauty of creation.

## Soul Reconnection

Soul Reconnection is a continuous process of returning to your true self, gently shedding the layers that hide your natural radiance. As you go through daily life, each breath and act of mindful awareness becomes a chance to rediscover the sacred spark within. By nurturing this inner connection, you build clarity, resilience, and deep compassion for yourself and others. This ongoing journey encourages you to honor your truth and embrace the fullness of who you are, creating a foundation for genuine healing and transformation that shines through every moment.

Every moment offers a chance to reconnect with your true self. Even during setbacks, paying attention to your breath and grounding yourself can help, reminding you of your inner strength. Through gentle self-compassion and openness, you make space for healing and growth.

Through this process, you realize that your journey isn't about becoming someone new but about reconnecting with the self that has always been within you. Every mindful pause and each conscious breath serve as gentle reminders of your innate wholeness and the steady presence of your soul. By honoring this inner light, you ignite a sense of peace and purpose that brightens every part of your life, fostering genuine connection with yourself and the world around you.

### Reflective Questions

- Where in my life do I feel disconnected from my true self?
- How can I reconnect with my divine nature?
- Which parts of my true essence feel hidden or overlooked?
- How does the ego or past conditioning shape my self-perception?
- What steps can I take today to reconnect with the divine spark inside me?

**Exercise: Quiet Reflection**

Take a few moments of peaceful stillness. Imagine yourself as pure essence—existing before any external form or identity. As you breathe deeply, feel the timeless and eternal light at the center of your being.

*Even after all this time*
*The sun never says to the earth,*
*"You owe Me."*
*Look what happens with*
*A love like that,*
*It lights the Whole Sky.*

*-Hafez*

# Chapter 9

## healing the root cause of separation and illness

*I am complete and whole. Divine light restores harmony within me.*

**Understanding the Origin of Illness**

The heart of all imbalances lies sorrow and soul loss, which originate from feeling disconnected from the divine spirit and your true self. This disconnection happens when you view yourself solely as a separate being. Such fragmentation interrupts the flow of life force and can eventually result in illness or disease. Recognizing this separation is the first step toward healing because restoration begins with a conscious return to wholeness. By acknowledging the unity between your soul and the divine spirit, you start the process of reconnecting with your true essence. This inner reunion allows the life force to flow freely, nourishing every part of your being. As you gently rebuild this connection, the layers of sorrow and loss begin to dissolve, creating space for harmony and vitality to flourish again within you.

**Steps Toward Healing:** Healing begins by reconnecting with your true self—seeing it as whole and complete—and embracing the journey of soul realization. When you view yourself through Divine Vision, your vibration naturally rises, freeing you from the limits of your past.

Dedicate daily time to meditation and prayer to strengthen your connection with your Divine Source. Take intentional steps to heal the past and remove energetic imprints from your energy body. Use the power of light to address your physical, mental, emotional, and spiritual layers.

### Working with Life Force Centers (Chakras)

Explore your life force centers, also known as chakras, and their emotional and mental aspects. By scanning each energy center, you can identify restrictions or blockages that hinder the flow of divine energy.

Use your breath as a tool: inhale divine healing light and exhale anything that doesn't reflect this light. Remember, your true nature is essential for your soul's growth into pure consciousness.

### The Energy Centers and Their Emotional Importance

Each chakra, or life force center, connects to specific emotions and life lessons. Working with these centers can help you identify and release energetic blockages, allowing divine energy to flow freely and support your overall healing process.

### Root Chakra: Fear and Foundation

The root chakra is associated with feelings of safety, security, and grounding. When it is balanced, it helps you feel stable and connected to life.

The affirmation for the root chakra is: I am safe, secure, and supported by life.

**Sacral Chakra: Self-Love and Creativity:** This chakra influences your self-esteem and creativity. It motivates you to embrace your uniqueness and express yourself artistically.

The affirmation for the sacral chakra is: I am abundant with life's creative energy, and my heart lives in unconditional self-love.

### Solar Plexus Chakra: Personal Power

Links to personal power, confidence, and independence. It helps you release limiting patterns and embrace the strength of your Divine Source.

The affirmation for the solar plexus chakra is: I release personal power and embrace the power of my Divine Source.

**Heart Chakra: Compassion and Connection:** The heart chakra is the center of love, compassion, and connection to others. Opening this chakra helps you find peace and rest in the silence of your sacred heart.

The affirmation for the heart chakra is: I rest in the silence of my sacred heart.

**Throat Chakra: Truth and Expression**

This chakra governs honest communication and self-expression. When balanced, it allows you to openly share your true self.

The affirmation for the throat chakra is: I express my authentic self.

**Third Eye Chakra: Intuition and Insight**

The link to intuition, insight, and inner guidance. Activating this center improves clarity and wisdom.

The affirmation for this chakra is: I open to Divine Healing Vision, seeing with clarity and insight.

**Crown Chakra: Integration and Unity**

The crown chakra links you to higher consciousness and unity with your source. It promotes a sense of connection and spiritual harmony.

The affirmation for this center: "I am connected to the divine wisdom within and around me."

**The Subtle Energy Fields**

The vital force moves within and around you, passing through various subtle energy fields.

**Emotional Field:** Connected to the root, navel, and solar plexus chakras, it reflects your feelings and emotional patterns. Healing this layer helps release past habits.

**Mental Field:** Related to the heart chakra, it encompasses your thoughts, beliefs, and intentions. Focusing on this area helps uncover hidden beliefs and align your thoughts with your soul's purpose.

**Spiritual Field:** Connected to the throat, third eye, crown, and soul star chakra, this links you to your divine essence, anchoring wisdom and light that guide your growth. Engaging with this field fosters a deeper integration of spiritual lessons.

**Reflective Questions**

- Where do I feel fragmented in my body, mind, or spirit?
- Which limiting beliefs or emotions am I willing to release?
- How can I reconnect with my inner sense of wholeness?

# guided practice for chakra awareness

Begin by taking a few deep, mindful breaths. With each inhale and exhale, direct your focus to the energy centers in your body, starting from the base and moving upward.

- Root Center: Breathe into the root center, positioned in the pelvic area and lower back. Notice any sensations or feelings in this fundamental energy center.
- Navel Center: Direct your focus to the area around your belly button. Breathe deeply and observe any movement or warmth in that spot.
- Solar Plexus Chakra: Direct your breath to the solar plexus, situated in the stomach area below your rib cage. Notice any emotions or energy flow in this region.

- Heart Center: Focus your awareness on the heart center, located within your chest cavity. As you breathe, notice any feelings of openness or resistance in this area.

- Throat Center: Focus your breath on the throat area, covering both the front and back parts. Notice any sensations or blockages as you breathe softly here.

- Third Eye Center: Focus your attention on the area between your eyebrows, known as the third eye. Notice any subtle impressions or changes in perception.

- Crown Center: Focus your attention on the crown of your head — the spot where a baby's soft spot is. Let your breath help you sense openness and lightness.

As you move through each center, maintain gentle, mindful breathing and notice any sensations, emotions, or areas that feel blocked. This practice aids healing light to flow through each chakra, gently clearing and restoring balance throughout your energy system.

*Run my dear,
From anything
That may not strengthen
Your precious budding wings.*

*Run like hell my dear,
From anyone likely
To put a sharp knife
Into the sacred, tender vision
Of your beautiful heart."
— Hafez*

# Chapter 10

# the sacred heart initiation— entering your inner sanctuary

*Within my heart, heaven and earth come together. Here, divine love shows its eternal rhythm—not just as an idea, but as a living fire.*

**The Temple Within**

Deep within each of us lies a chamber of quiet brilliance, the sacred heart. It is more than just a symbol; it is a living sanctuary where divine and human consciousness come together. When you enter this inner temple, you go beyond separation and stop looking for love outside yourself. Instead, you realize that love is your true essence.

The Sacred Heart is a refuge for your inner self. Here, judgment transforms into compassion, and every wound becomes an opportunity for grace.

**The Fire of Divine Love:** Initiation into the sacred heart is not a one-time event but an ongoing journey. Every challenge, sorrow, and act of surrender gradually breaks down the barriers around your heart until love becomes your instinctive response to life.

Divine love doesn't require you to be invulnerable; it encourages you to stay open. It moves through your vulnerability, transforming pain into wisdom and longing into prayer. When you allow this sacred fire to flow through you, it doesn't destroy but lights the way.

**Living from the Heart**

Living from the sacred heart means flowing smoothly through each experience and transforming emotions with awareness. When anger arises, breathe love into it. When sadness appears, tend to it gently. When joy manifests, let it flow freely. The Heart initiation teaches us

to view each emotion as a divine message and every relationship as a sacred mirror. The heart becomes your guide, helping you respond to life with love.

**Remember Who You Are:** During the Sacred Heart initiation, the call to "remember who you are" encourages you to reconnect with your true self. This isn't about discovering something that was lost, but about realizing that love is already part of who you are.

This remembrance isn't about striving for perfection or seeking validation from others. Instead, it's about allowing your presence to turn judgment into compassion and transform wounds into grace.

The Sacred Heart Initiation isn't about becoming divine; it's about realizing that you already are. With this awareness, every breath becomes a prayer, every encounter turns into a blessing, and every heartbeat whispers the truth: "Love is not something I seek. Love is what I am."

### Your Inner Lotus—The Seat of Your Soul

Your Inner Lotus blooms at the heart's sanctuary, gently unfolding as you surrender to the present moment and embrace your divine nature. Here, the sacred wisdom within your heart unites with the innocence of your inner child, allowing a more profound sense of unity and belonging will emerge.

As you nurture this inner lotus through moments of stillness and conscious intention, its petals unfold to reveal the radiant essence of your soul, inviting divine guidance to illuminate each step of your journey.

### Sacred Practice: The Heart Flame Meditation

- Sit quietly and place your hand on your heart.
- Allow your breathing to slow and steady.
- Feel a warm, golden light shining inside your chest.

- With each inhale, imagine this warm light filling your whole body.

- Silently repeat: "I open to the sacred fire of love. May this flame purify, heal, and guide me."

- Stay in this bright space for a few minutes.

**Affirmation:** *"My heart is the altar of divine love. Through openness, I become the living expression of grace."*

**Reflective Questions**

- How receptive is my heart to divine guidance?

- What past experiences or ego patterns might stop you from fully surrendering?

- How can I nurture innocence and inner peace?

**Heart-Centered Exercise**

Spend five minutes focusing on your heart center. As you breathe, picture a golden light growing brighter with each inhale. Let this light dissolve any resistance, making space for divine love to flow in.

*"This is love: to fly toward a secret sky, to cause a hundred veils to fall each moment"*

-Rumi

# Chapter 11

## ascension—your soul's calling

*I honor my soul's journey and elevate into my divine purpose with grace.*

**Soul's Journey Through Dimensions**

As your soul journeys through different dimensions, each level presents unique lessons and growth opportunities. These experiences are meant to help you release limiting beliefs and awaken your true spiritual potential. By attentively listening to your inner wisdom, you can navigate these dimensions with clarity and purpose, viewing each challenge as a catalyst for greater expansion.

Before birth, your soul enters Earth's school, initiating a profound transformation of your sacred creative energy. Once awakened, Earth's school becomes a lesson in empowerment—an opportunity to choose between serving the Light or the ego. The path you select involves activating your soul's power and aligning with higher will, which is deeply connected to the frequencies of God: Love, Light, and Truth.

**Challenges on the Path to Ascension**

Every soul is called to achieve its highest potential. However, many stray from this sacred path due to a lack of support. The world often promotes ego, identity, and status, which can block spiritual growth. The daily fight to survive leaves many exhausted, and doubt, fear, and mistrust can lead them to abandon their true calling.

For those committed to ascension, dedication is essential for overcoming obstacles—both personal and collective—many of which come from ancestral conditioning.

### Daily Sacred Practice and Remembrance

Every day becomes a sacred act of remembering your true essence and forgiving mistakes caused by false identification. Healing the ego can be difficult and may require revisiting patterns from past lives. Through sacred remembrance, you deepen your understanding of your soul and return to the bliss of your true nature.

During this sacred journey, it's important to cultivate compassion for yourself and others. Gently accepting your imperfections lets you grow without judgment and builds stronger bonds with those around you. By practicing patience and grace, you create space for inner transformation and foster a loving environment for your soul's growth.

### Transforming Patterns and Elevating Frequency

Limiting patterns develop in the body's energy centers. By learning to scan your energy field, you can identify where these patterns are. Frequency medicine raises the vibration of these patterns, transforming fear into love.

Each frequency trapped in your energy system functions as a time capsule, waiting to be opened by divine frequencies. By practicing daily mindfulness, you can identify where these lower patterns are stored, breathe divine frequencies into them, and gradually fill your energy body with healing light.

### Clearing the Ascension Passageway

For ascension, it is vital to clear the passage so divine energy can flow freely upward through your multidimensional aura. When you practice "Soul Love," you dedicate time each day to expressing gratitude in prayer. Every breath becomes a gift of grace, reminding you of the love that you are.

**Living from the Heart and Sacred Silence:** Your daily life centers around your heart, the vital organ of your body and the inner sanctuary of

your soul. This sanctuary is safeguarded by the sacred light of silence. In silence, you can express your highest truth and essence.

Each day provides an opportunity to look inward and see, with Divine Healing Vision, what needs to be activated for you to align with your sacred life order.

**Awakening Your Inner Divine Lotus:** Through your ascension, you connect with the vastness of your infinite nature and embrace your birthright—the 1000-petal Lotus. This divine lotus links you to all your past lives, uniting every experience into a single force of love and light.

This blooming of the inner lotus inspires deep wisdom to flow into your awareness, illuminating even the darkest corners of your mind. As your divine lotus unfolds, you may notice a strong sense of unity with all beings and a gentle release of old attachments. Let this expansive love radiate outward, blessing every part of your life and the world around you.

## Opening Your Soul Star: The Eighth Chakra

The soul star, also called the eighth chakra, is located above the crown of your head and acts as a gateway to your higher self and divine wisdom. Opening the soul star involves setting intentions to connect with your highest aspects, inviting the purest light to flow into your energy field. Spend quiet moments in meditation, focusing your awareness just above your head, and visualize a radiant sphere of light blooming and expanding.

As you intentionally connect with your soul star, you may experience a deep sense of peace and a stronger spiritual purpose. Let this connection help you release old limitations, embrace new insights, and fully step onto your soul's path. With each breath, draw divine energy through this chakra, allowing it to fill your entire being with love and clarity.

The soul star chakra not only serves as a gateway to your higher self and divine wisdom, but it is also closely linked to the Akashic Records. These records are viewed as a vast, multidimensional library containing the energetic imprint of every soul's journey—past, present, and future. By activating and opening your soul star, you establish a connection to these sacred records, granting access to deep spiritual knowledge and lessons gathered over many lifetimes.

During meditation, focus on the space above your head and set the intention to connect with the Akashic Records through your soul star. You might receive subtle insights, visions, or intuitive guidance that help clarify your soul's purpose and reveal patterns that are ready for healing. This connection allows you to approach your spiritual growth with more wisdom, compassion, and clarity, drawing from the endless well of your soul's history to guide your current path. As you explore the formless soul star within you, radiating divine potential and an eternal connection to God, you honor your soul's sacred promise: to become a beacon of Light and Love, healing and transforming the world.

**Reflective Questions**

- What is my soul's highest calling?
- What patterns or limitations prevent me from stepping into it?
- How can I honor divine timing in my spiritual growth?

**Soul Awakening Exercise- The Heart of Witnessing**

Begin by selecting one limiting pattern you've noticed in yourself. Find a quiet space, sit comfortably, and focus on your breath. Allow each inhale to bring awareness to the pattern, imagining it being infused with a higher energy frequency. As you breathe in, visualize this pattern being illuminated and transformed.

With each exhale, consciously release any lingering resistance related to this pattern. Let go of past energies and allow yourself to feel lighter and more open with every breath.

Return to this practice regularly, supporting your journey with the following affirmation: "I am open to divine guidance and surrender to my soul's highest calling."

*All doubt, despair, and fear become insignificant when the intention of life becomes love.*

*-Rumi*

# Chapter 12

## transformation is the work of a light being

*I surrender to divine light, blending my human experience with my soul's essence.*

### The Path to Discovering Your Divine Soul

Transformation is a deep and complex journey that involves releasing years of conditioning to connect with your divine soul. This process is similar to alchemy, requiring the integrating of your everyday human experiences with the essence of your eternal soul.

The foundation of transformation is unity consciousness. By choosing unity, you plant the seed for meaningful change, releasing inner duality and connecting to your core—where darkness and light are not separate but flow together as one radiant light.

As unity consciousness forms the foundation from which transformation arises, you naturally become open to surrender and the flow of divine light. In this space of integration, true transformation begins as the line between shadow and illumination fades away. Surrendering connects you to the infinite source, freeing your inner divine child from ego restrictions and old stories. No longer defined by opposites or the weight of history, you become receptive to the unconditional energy of the divine, where appreciation for all experiences deepens and the journey of awakening unfolds in harmony.

**Surrender and the Flow of Divine Light**

True transformation starts with surrendering to the divine. Through surrender, you connect your consciousness with divine light, freeing your inner divine child from the stories and chains of the ego.

Right now, you realize that you are more than just a self defined by history or opposites. When you surrender, you open yourself to the unconditional flow of divine energy, allowing you to deeply appreciate all life experiences.

**Returning to Divine Frequency:** As you grow, you start reconnecting with the angelic realm and the God Frequency, where your purpose is to serve. You become aware of the stories you've been part of or lost yourself in, and these now call for your compassion and, when needed, forgiveness.

This journey is characterized by humility, compassion, longing, and occasional grief as you observe suffering and the passage of time. Still, you are led forward by angelic Grace.

Raising your frequency from fear to love means intentionally shifting how you feel and interpret your emotions. It encourages you to go beyond fear's boundaries and embrace love's expansive energy.

This transformation begins with mindfulness during moments of anxiety, doubt, or separation, viewing them as chances to nurture compassion and reconnect with your divine essence. Through intentional breathwork, affirmations, and gentle release of old patterns, you invite love's vibration to fill your being, dissolving fear's shadows and waking your inner healing light.

**The Power of Soul Intention, Affirmation, and Release.**

Affirming your divine potential is important. Use affirmations like: "I release all worry and concern in this timeline. I release fear of loss, pain of loss, and grieving heartbreaks."

By mastering the lessons of your soul, you honor both your body and your life. The soul's medicine involves elevating your energy to a higher vibration, releasing lower emotions, and healing patterns of suffering.

As you breathe in, invite self-love to fill your energy and dissolve stagnation. As you breathe out, release feelings of abandonment and embrace the joy of your true self. Affirm new beginnings with gratitude, and let go of thoughts and labels that reinforce old patterns.

**Empowerment and the Sacred Heart**

Recognize your divine empowerment and understand that the lost soul or inner child may sometimes seek control. Let go of the craving for power and instead surrender to your ever-present, unbroken divine soul.

The Sacred Heart is your inner temple, the home for your true nature. Take time to focus on the Sacred Heart, listening to its quiet voice and feeling the vibration of unconditional love. This inner sanctuary connects you to God; care for it by releasing tension and dedicating moments to being present.

**Reclaim Your Voice and Activate Divine Healing**

As you advance in your journey toward reaching your highest potential, you reclaim parts of yourself that were silenced or afraid to speak the truth. Trust your inner voice; sometimes, silence itself nourishes your being. Seek guidance from your intuition, your soul, and divine records.

Activate your "Divine Healing Vision" by viewing your life through intuition and imagining your soul's radiant, luminous core. Visualize your soul as a vibration field, and train your mind to see the sacredness in all beings, honoring unity over division.

**The Alchemy of Transformation**

Ultimately, transformation is the power of both human experience and divine essence. It starts with surrender, dissolves duality, and merges darkness and light into a single, radiant whole.

By practicing humility, compassion, forgiveness, and gratitude, you elevate your vibration and draw in the unconditional flow of divine light. The Sacred Heart serves as your gateway to presence, helping you reclaim lost parts of yourself and see life clearly, guided by unity and divine consciousness.

**Reflective Questions**

- What is the purpose of my soul?
- What habits are preventing me from making progress?
- How can I honor the timing of my growth?

**Transformative Exercise**

Choose one habit that hinders your progress. As you take deep breaths, visualize this habit transforming into a positive force. With each inhale, embrace change and renewal; with each exhale, release old patterns and welcome growth.

*Let yourself be silently drawn by the strange pull of what you really love. It will not lead you astray.*

*-Rumi*

# Chapter 13

## trusting your source

*I trust the divine within me. I am guided, supported, and loved infinitely.*

### The Nature of Trust

To foster trust in the source of existence, remember that you are a beloved child of the Divine. Trust naturally grows from a heart filled with devotion. However, when the heart is cluttered with thoughts and feelings rooted in the personal self, authentic trust can be challenging to establish.

### The Challenge of Trust

Trusting in your Divine source can be challenging because life is temporary and always changing. The world's fleeting and unpredictable nature often causes doubt. This constant flux makes it difficult to feel confident about what we observe around us.

Despite the challenge, remember that uncertainty can also serve as an invitation to deepen your connection with the Divine. By gently observing your doubts instead of fighting them, you create space for greater trust to grow. Each moment of uncertainty becomes an opportunity to renew your faith and open your heart to guidance.

### The Sacred Act of Surrender

Trust is like a delicate flower that blooms when we're willing to let go. This process is a sacred act of releasing attachment to the physical world and the ego. As we surrender, the heart opens and becomes receptive, allowing the gentle presence of the Divine to nurture us from within. In letting go, we discover a deeper innocence—a quiet strength that grounds us beyond the world's constant changes. Through this surrender, our trust grows, giving us the courage to face

each moment with faith and the reassurance that our true essence is held in infinite love.

**Returning to Innocence**

By remembering you are a child of the Divine and letting go of attachments, you reconnect with your pure, innocent self. Then, trust becomes the foundation that allows you to awaken to your true nature inside.

Accepting uncertainty is a vital part of the spiritual journey because it teaches us resilience and deepens our connection with the Divine. When we allow ourselves to lean into vulnerability, we find a profound sense of peace that comes from trusting something greater than ourselves. This trust encourages us to keep moving forward, even when the path isn't clear, knowing that every experience provides a chance for spiritual growth.

**Walking in Trust**

With trust, you navigate life as if holding God's hand—feeling safe, supported, and never alone. Anything that fosters mistrust or deceit in the world does not belong to the divine realm. By surrendering and choosing to connect with God, you let go of the lower vibrations of ego and false self. As you continue walking in trust, remember that each step you take is an act of faith inviting the Divine to walk with you. During times of doubt or confusion, pause and reconnect with your inner guidance, allowing it to gently lead you back to peace. Recognizing the support available to you, both seen and unseen, can strengthen your sense of safety and belonging on your journey.

**Living in Infinite Love**

Your true nature is an infinite love that exists beyond the temporary limits of the personal self or physical world. Trust who you are and let it guide you at every step. Trust also encourages us to view each moment as sacred, reminding us that every experience holds a lesson for our growth. By releasing our need to control, we allow greater wisdom to lead us and bring purpose to our lives. In this openness, we understand that trust is not passive — it is a deliberate choice to align ourselves with the flow of love and grace, even when facing the unknown.

When you choose to trust, you connect with wisdom that surpasses the limits of thought and circumstance. This connection brings peace and clarity, even during uncertain times. Trusting the Divine is an ongoing practice—one that develops through gentle patience and self-compassion, helping you navigate life with openness and grace.

### Soul Affirmation

*I trust the divine within me. I am guided, supported, and loved infinitely.*

### Reflective Questions

- Where do I find it hardest to trust?
- How can I develop faith and surrender?

### Building Trust From Within

Practice daily affirmations and mindful breathing to strengthen your trust in your source energy. Regularly affirm your intention to trust, and use conscious breathing to stay centered in the present, allowing trust to grow naturally.

As you grow more confident in the infinite love within you, you naturally become more surrendering and open to life's unfolding mysteries. This inner development helps you appreciate each moment, trusting that divine wisdom is always guiding you. Over time, trust becomes effortless—an unshakable foundation that supports you through both joy and challenges.

*Do not climb the difficult stairs of fear to God. Take the comfortable elevator to God. – St Therese of Lisieux*

# Chapter 14

## witnessing light—living in divine trust

*In moments of stillness, I observe the light flowing through everything. I trust the rhythm, timing, and grace of this light because it is the heartbeat of creation within me.*

**The Grace of Witnessing**

The light of your soul perceives your life experiences through love, compassion, and forgiveness. The personal self is often hidden beneath layers of mental and emotional conditioning. At the core of your awareness is the witness, an aspect of yourself that is always present and loving.

Awareness itself is love, and love is the act of divine healing vision. When you witness through the source, your very act of witnessing becomes a healing force. Each day offers an opportunity for spiritual growth. This journey encourages you to shift your awareness, allowing you to see through divine perspective. To achieve this, release mental judgments, conditioned patterns, and the layers of misidentification linked to the separate sense of self.

Witnessing Light is not just about observing life, but also about practicing letting go and allowing your highest self to guide your perceptions gently. By cultivating this openness, you learn to recognize the subtle presence of grace woven through every experience, regardless of circumstances. This perspective helps you respond to life with compassion, patience, and quiet faith in the unfolding journey.

**Witnessing as an Act of Love**

Your soul's light perceives life through love, compassion, and forgiveness. The inner witness—pure awareness—serves as a healer by simply observing. Each day offers opportunities for soul realization.

As you release judgments, conditioning, and misidentifications, you reconnect with your eternal essence. Seeing through Divine Healing Vision allows you to shed temporary layers of identity and return to the boundless waters of your being. Witnessing then becomes an act of love and healing. Seeing the Divine Healing Vision helps you stop searching for signs or proof of divinity because you see it everywhere. In every breath, face, and passing moment, you recognize the same radiant essence guiding your path.

**Surrender to the Divine Rhythm**

Life unfolds according to its own wisdom—a rhythm older than time. Living in divine trust involves aligning yourself with that rhythm, letting your actions, words, and thoughts flow in harmony with it. There is peace in not knowing every answer, freedom in releasing expectations, and beauty in simply allowing events to unfold. Trust isn't passivity; it's a partnership with the unseen. By acting with faith and letting go with gratitude, life becomes an effortless dance of giving and receiving.

By adopting this approach, you might notice a subtle shift in your inner world, where everyday life becomes more meaningful. As you cultivate stillness and openness, your soul's wisdom surfaces, offering insight, comfort, and a sense of connection to something greater. Through mindful observation, you foster change not only within yourself but also in the world around you.

**Becoming the Living Light**

The journey of Divine Healing Vision isn't about transcending life but about fully embodying it. You become a living expression of everything you've witnessed—a vessel for grace.

To witness light is to embody it: walking softly on the earth, recognizing holiness in everyday moments, and bringing peace to every conversation, silence, and decision. Divine trust ceases to be just a practice and becomes your natural state once resistance disappears. From this awareness, even the simplest acts become sacred—a smile, a breath, or a moment of listening. Through you, light continues its eternal work of healing and transformation.

The path to healing and ascension is an inward journey that reminds you that the Divine has always been with you. Seeing light means living in love, breathing in peace, and trusting someone who already knows they are home.

*Everything is unfolding as it should. I see the light—and in my trust, the world feels whole.*

## Soul Reflection and Meditation

**Affirmation:** *"I am the witness of my life, observing with love, clarity, and compassion."*

### Reflective Questions

- How can I observe without making judgments?
- What insights come up when I see my life with love and awareness?

### Practical Exercise

Set aside time to sit quietly and notice your thoughts, feelings, and physical sensations as they come up. During this meditation, repeat the affirmation: "I witness my life with love and clarity." Let your awareness grow, observing each experience without attachment or judgment.

As you finish your meditation, gently redirect your attention back to the present moment. Notice any feelings of peace or clarity that arise, and see these as signs of your soul's gentle growth. Carry this loving awareness with you throughout the day, allowing it to shape your actions and interactions. Remember, even after your meditation ends, you can always return to this observing state, grounding yourself in compassion and presence.

### The Heart of Witnessing

At the core of witnessing is a sincere openness—a readiness to observe both yourself and the world without judgment or expectation. This gentle awareness enables you to see beyond surface appearances

and recognize the divine unfolding in each moment. Simply being present opens space for healing and growth, respecting life as it is and encouraging deeper understanding.

Witnessing is not passive; it is an act of loving attention that bridges separation, highlighting the sacred in both joy and challenge. In this state, your awareness becomes a vessel for peace, compassion, and clarity, guiding you to respond with kindness and wisdom. The essence of witnessing, then, is a continuous practice of seeing through the eyes of love and embracing each experience as a teacher on your soul's journey.

*What was said to the rose that made it open was said to me here in my chest.*

*- Rumi*

# Chapter 15

## the art of soul love

Soul love is at the core of our being and inspires our journey through different levels of energy and awareness. Each day encourages us to trust in our soul's unique path, recognizing this sacred space as the place where we grow into our true, authentic selves. Life constantly offers new opportunities to start fresh and remember our true nature—that we are not limited to body, mind, or emotions, but are eternal beings of light.

To truly love your soul is to nurture it like a small child inside, caring for it with consistent devotion and tenderness. Regularly resting in your heart allows you to experience the rhythm of your true essence, which blends love, beauty, and truth. As you tend to your soul's inner garden, you'll notice more beauty blooming in harmony with the rhythm of your soul's light. Trust in your inner light to guide and nurture your inner garden by gently releasing the burdens of the ego, attachments, and the built sense of self. By giving yourself the love you need, you open the path to rise toward your highest soul's frequency, remembering that your journey is one of ongoing growth and unity with the Divine.

Soul love is a daily practice—nurturing your inner being with divine frequencies and clearing away anything that does not reflect this sacred essence, which is your true nature. This ongoing process involves releasing discordant energy and aligning with your unobstructed core light. Resting in the presence of your Sacred Heart allows you to experience the fullness of your soul's love.

**Loving Awareness**

When you connect with soul love, you naturally brighten every part of your experience with compassion and understanding. This loving

awareness helps break down barriers between yourself and others, inviting a sense of unity and peace into daily life. Over time, you may notice more ease in forgiving, accepting, and embracing who you truly are, as well as those around you.

This loving awareness is not just a gentle light but also a powerful spark for growth. By embracing each moment with openness and compassion, you allow healing energies to flow freely, nurturing deeper connections within yourself and with others. As you cultivate this practice, you'll begin to feel a stronger sense of unity and purpose, guided by the wisdom of your soul's love.

**Love and freedom**

As soulful love deepens, it changes our view, inspiring us to live with a sense of completeness and acceptance. During hard times, this love acts as a gentle guide, urging us to reconnect with our hearts and honor our true selves. Through daily presence and dedication, we build a sanctuary within where love, wisdom, and compassion thrive.

Through this conscious presence, your heart becomes a vessel for both giving and receiving unconditional love. As you deepen your connection to soul love, you'll find freedom that comes from releasing expectations and embracing life as it unfolds. This openness brings a profound sense of joy and fulfillment, rooted in the understanding that your true essence is love.

**I Am the Vessel of Divine Light and Vision.**

Embracing soul love also leads us into a more profound silence within ourselves—a sacred space where the mind finds peace and the heart listens without judgment. In this silence, we become aware of what is truly out of sync, gently observing our thoughts and feelings as they arise. With patience and presence, we welcome the process of awakening to our true home inside, guided by the healing vision that sees the soul as pure love, always present and steady.

During these moments of stillness, invite your soul's light to gently illuminate any area needing healing or clarity. Notice the subtle shifts in your energy as you open yourself to the nourishing presence of unconditional love. Allow yourself to rest in this sacred awareness, trusting that each breath brings you closer to the truth of who you are—whole, radiant, and deeply connected to the Divine.

**Soul Love Through Compassion and Forgiveness**

Connecting with the love of your soul naturally fosters compassion and understanding in all areas of your life. This compassionate awareness helps break down barriers that separate you from others, encouraging unity and peace in your daily life. As you develop this practice, you might find it easier to forgive, accept, and embrace both yourself and those around you.

As the depth of soulful love deepens, it changes your perceptions, motivating you to engage with life from a sense of wholeness and acceptance. In tough times, this love functions as a gentle guide, reminding you to return to your heart and honor your true nature. Through mindful presence and daily devotion, you create an inner sanctuary where love, wisdom, and compassion flourish.

By releasing discordant energies and aligning with your core light, you create a space where forgiveness and compassion flow naturally. This ongoing process helps you experience greater freedom by letting go of expectations and embracing life as it unfolds. Rooted in this loving presence, you find joy and fulfillment, knowing that your true essence is love.

As you continue nurturing soul love, you'll notice this inner transformation gradually spreading outward, impacting your relationships and environment. The peace and acceptance you cultivate become a guiding light, inspiring others to open their hearts and embrace a more compassionate way of being. In this way, your journey not only heals and uplifts you but also promotes greater harmony in the world.

**Soul Love Meditation and Reflection**

Soul Love Meditation and Reflection gently encourages you to pause and reconnect with your inner sanctuary, allowing the wisdom and compassion gained through soulful love to permeate your consciousness fully. As you settle into silent awareness, feel the natural flow of breath guiding you deeper into the heart, where acceptance and forgiveness awaken. In this sacred space, let your reflections come naturally without judgment—witnessing thoughts and sensations with kindness as you align with your true essence. Each moment spent in mindful meditation strengthens your connection to the divine, clearing the way for clarity and peace to emerge. By regularly nurturing this practice, you build a stable foundation from which your highest vision and purpose can unfold, supporting your ongoing journey of growth, surrender, and awakening. Embrace these moments of reflection not only as healing pauses but as stepping stones toward embodying love and illuminating your path forward.

**Integrating the Light Within**

Your journey through Divine Healing Vision is a continuous process of awakening, surrender, and growth. The insights, reflections, and practices shared here act as tools to help you align your soul, mind, and body, supporting you as you embody your highest vision at every moment.

Remember, transformation isn't a straight path. Challenges, growth, and clarity often go hand in hand, each teaching valuable lessons for your soul's development. By embracing the present, trusting the divine, and cultivating conscious awareness, you deepen your connection to your sacred purpose and divine potential. Keep practicing intuition, releasing control, aligning, and observing. Let your Sacred Heart lead you, guiding your thoughts, words, and actions with love, compassion, and authenticity.

The journey doesn't end with the last page — it continues through every breath, decision, and interaction. Your divine core is

eternal, and as you live with awareness and surrender, you illuminate not only your path but also the world around you.

May your heart remain open, your vision stay clear, and your spirit shine brightly. Walk your sacred path with faith, courage, and love, knowing you are supported, guided, and endlessly cherished by the Divine.

*Your task is not to seek love, but merely to seek and find all barriers within yourself that you have built against it.*

*-Rumi*

# Conclusion

## Affirmation

*I walk my sacred path with love, light, and unwavering faith.*

## The Ongoing Journey

This journey is not limited to a single moment or chapter; it continues with every breath and decision. By practicing daily habits such as meditation, affirmations, and reflection, you deepen your connection to your soul, build trust, and remain aligned with divine guidance. Each moment provides another opportunity to embody your highest vision and live according to your sacred purpose.

## Remembering Your True Essence

This book serves as a gentle reminder of your true nature. As you move forward, you may see light in every face and hear love in all you meet. Trust in the rhythm of grace unfolding within you, letting it guide your thoughts, words, and actions.

## Living in Divine Trust and Love

Walking your path in divine trust means embracing each step with unwavering faith in the guidance that surrounds you. Let your life reflect love, radiating kindness and compassion in everything you do. You are the light, constantly reminding yourself of your brilliance and purpose.

## A Vessel of Light and Remembrance

May this offering serve as a vessel of light, awakening the remembrance of your true self within your heart and the hearts of others. Through healing of the heart, let it guide all beings toward wholeness and lasting

peace. In this sacred space, unity, healing, and the gentle unfolding of love's presence are always available.

## Beloved Traveler of Light

Your journey has been a sacred passage from vision to realization, and from seeking to remembrance. With each chapter, you have gently shed layers of illusion and rediscovered the wholeness within yourself. This path is not about becoming something more; it is about returning home to your authentic essence. Every step has been guided by the Divine, shifting your awareness from external distractions to the sanctuary within. Through this process, you have reclaimed the radiant stillness of your true self.

## A New Beginning

As you close these pages, a new beginning begins. The teachings have become part of you, living in your heart and soul. Every breath, heartbeat, and quiet moment is an opportunity to return to love. Moving forward, walk gently upon the earth, carrying the energy of peace. Let your words be blessings, your thoughts prayers, and your actions gentle in motion. Even in silence, your presence will speak—a living reminder of the Divine within every being.

## Connection to Source

If you ever lose sight of this truth, place your hand on your heart and feel the rhythm of creation within you. Breathe deeply and softly affirm your soul: I am connected to Source. I am whole. I am at peace.

## Divine Guidance Throughout Life

Always remember that you are a child of God. Listen for the subtle whisper of Divine guidance within your soul through every season of life. May this guidance soften what is rigid, illuminate what is hidden, and awaken what is eternal within you. You are the living light of Divine

Healing Vision—a reflection of love in motion, a vessel of grace, and a witness to the infinite.

## Namaste, Dear Reader,

Jaya Sarada is a highly experienced energy healer, author, and teacher of ancient wisdom. With many years dedicated to energy healing and spiritual growth, she has committed herself to helping others discover their inner potential and reconnect with their divine essence.

### Journey and Background

Jaya's journey began with an early calling to explore and learn from sacred healing practices around the world. These transformative experiences helped her develop a deep understanding of the complex connection between mind, body, and spirit. This knowledge forms the foundation for the energy work she shares with others today.

### Healing Methods and Services

Throughout her career, Jaya has created several unique healing methods. Her services include the Life Essence Awakening Process (L.E.A.P.), Energy Testing and Clearing, Chakra Healing, and Sound Healing with Guided Meditations. She also practices Integrated Energy Therapy (I.E.T.). Jaya offers these sessions remotely and provides intuitive readings, such as Akashic Record Readings, Oracle Readings, and Tarot Readings. These services aim to promote spiritual clarity and alignment with the soul's purpose. Jaya Sarada is an ordained minister from Pathways of Light with a solid foundation in *A Course in Miracles*.

### Books and Publications

Jaya is also a skilled author. She has written several books focused on empowering individuals, energy healing practitioners, and healthcare professionals to integrate energy healing into their personal and professional lives. Her publications include:

- Well Being in Body, Mind, and Spirit

- Trust in Yourself: The Path to Awakening
- Awakening Your Chakras: A Magical Journey of Transformation
- The Path of Return: A Guide for Sacred Living
- Living Meditations
- Divine Soul Empowerment
- The Sacred Path of Peace
- The Sacred Path of Love
- Divine Healing Vision-The Art of Vibrational Well-Being

NOT

## Community Work and Foundation

Jaya Sarada is the founder of Divine Light Foundation, a nonprofit organization dedicated to providing financial support for healing, awakening, and transformation. To learn more about this initiative, please visit www.divinelightfoundation.org. For additional details about her personal services, visit

www.divinehealingvision.com.

Email: jaya@divinehealingvision.com.

## Contact Information for Divine Light Publishing

Divine Light Publishing can be reached by mail or phone.

PO Box 1110 Gleneden Beach, Oregon 97388

For inquiries or further information, please call the toll-free number:

1-855-505-3935

www.ingramcontent.com/pod-product-compliance
Lightning Source LLC
LaVergne TN
LVHW010030070426
835512LV00004B/50